Waffles, Flapjacks, Pancakes, Blintzes, Crêpes, Frybread from Scandinavia and Around the World
Revised and Expanded

Compiled by Dianna Stevens

Edited by Miriam Canter; Associate Editors: Pat Birk, Dorothy Crum, Joan Liffring-Zug Bourret

John Zu

Cover Design by Es

About the Compiler and Food Editor

Dianna Stevens, compiler, is a journalism graduate of Northwestern University and has assisted with the production of many Penfield books. She loves to cook for her husband, Trey, and their pancake-loving children, Alexandra, MacPherson, and Annabella.

Miriam Canter, editor, loves cookbooks and cooking. Miriam, who has edited Penfield cookbooks since 1979, has written three cookbooks and has edited more than thirty.

ISBN 1-932043-10-1
©2002 Penfield Books ©1992 Penfield Press

Contents

PANCAKES 6

Pancakes Around the World 7

Pancake Tips 9

Apple-Cottage Cheese Pancakes 10

Applesauce Pancakes 11

Baked Polish Pancakes with Apple Filling 12

Banana Pancakes 14

Basic Buttermilk Pancakes 15

Buttermilk Pancake Variations 16

Blini (Russian Pancakes) 17

Buckwheat Pancakes 18

Cheesy Potato Pancakes 19

Chocolate Pancakes 20

Corn Pancakes 21

Czech Featherweight Pancakes 22

Danish Pancakes 23

Dutch Baby 24

Poffertjes (Dutch Mini-Pancakes) 25

Finnish Pancakes with Cranberry Sauce 26

Flapjacks 27

German Baked Apple Pancake 28

Gingerbread Pancakes 30

Greek Pancakes with Honey Syrup 31

Hearty Molasses Hotcakes 32

Hungarian Pancakes 33

Icelandic Pancakes 34

Indian Fried Bread 35

Jewish Potato *Latkes* 37

Johnnycakes 38

Chinese Mandarin Pancakes 39

Matzo Meal Pancakes 40

Norwegian Cottage Cheese Pancakes 41

Panqueque de Alejandro (Chilean Pancakes) . . 42

Peanut Butter Pancakes 43

Popover Pancake 44

Puffy Danish Pancake 45

Pumpkin Pancakes	46
Raisin Buttermilk Pancakes	47
Shrovetide Pancakes	48
Spicy Apple Pancakes with Cider Sauce	49
Spinach Pancakes	51
Swedish Oven Pancake	52
Swedish Pancakes	53
Wisconsin-Swiss Pancakes	54
WAFFLES	55
Waffle Tips	57
Bacon and Cheese Waffles	58
Basic Waffles	59
Basic Waffle Variations	60
Belgian Waffles	61
Brownie Waffle Cookies	62
Cheesy Waffles	63
Coconut Waffles	64
Dutch Waffles	65
Finnish Waffles	66
French *Gaufres*	67
Gingerbread Waffles	68
Overnight Yeast Waffles	69
Peach Waffles	70
Potato Waffles	71
Raisin Oatmeal Waffles	72
Rice Flour Waffles	73
Rice Waffles	74
Rich Waffles	75
Southern Grits Waffles	76
Swedish Waffles	77
Sweet Potato Waffles	78
Whole-Wheat Waffles	79
CRÊPES AND BLINTZES	80
How to Make Crêpes	81
Crêpe Tips	82
How to Fold Crêpes	83
Basic Crêpe Batter	84
Blueberry Blintzes	85

Cheese Blintzes .87	White Wine Chicken Crêpes 107
Chocolate Crêpes 89	Zucchini Crêpes 108
Finnish Crêpes .90	TOPPINGS AND SYRUPS 109
Finnish Oatmeal Crêpes 91	Fruit Syrup 110
French Soufflé Crêpes 92	Blueberry Cinnamon Syrup 111
Herb Crêpes 93	Blueberry Sauce 111
Lemon Crêpes .94	Lemon Applesauce/Apple Cinnamon Sauce . .112
Parmesan Cheese Crêpes 95	Brandy Maple Syrup/Orange Maple Syrup . .113
Potato Blintzes .96	Brown Sugar Syrup 114
Potato Crêpes 97	Orange Honey Syrup 114
Whole-Wheat Crêpes 98	Belgian Cream .115
Crêpe Fillings 99	Cinnamon Sour Cream Sauce 115
Apple Filling 100	Honey Butter 116
Apricot Brandy Crêpes 101	Banana Honey Butter 116
Italian Crêpes .102	Honey Spread 116
Potato Filling with Parmesan Cheese 103	Butterscotch Sauce/Chocolate Sauce 117
Raspberry Filling 104	Ham and Corn Topping/Meat Topping 118
Scallop Mushroom Crêpes 105	

Johnnycakes   *Plätter* (Swedish)

Flannel Cakes   *Po-ping* (Chinese)

Hoe Cakes   *Blini* (Russia and Poland)

Pancakes

Palacsinta (Hungarian)   Flapjacks

Pfannkuchen (German)   Griddle Cakes

Crêpe (French)   *Pannekoeke* (Dutch)

Pancakes Around the World

Many people think of pancakes as a lumberjack's hearty breakfast or a Sunday morning feast—golden cakes stacked high, soaked with butter and maple syrup, warm, delicious, and all-American. Although beloved by Americans, pancakes are universal and ancient. The unleavened pancake is possibly the oldest form of bread, needing only a grain, a liquid, and a very hot rock to cook on. Almost every country has a version of pancakes, and they aren't limited to breakfast.

American pioneers cooked their pancakes on the flat blades of their hoes over a hot fire, hence the name Hoe Cakes. Johnnycakes may have been known first as Shawnee Cakes, a Native-American pancake using cornmeal. Another theory on Johnnycakes is that they were originally called "Journey" Cakes because travelers often packed a bundle of them for trips, and settlers cooked them while on long treks. Flannel Cakes perhaps got their name from the flannel shirts pancake-eating lumberjacks wore.

continued

Pancakes *continued*

In England, Shrovetide Tuesday (the Tuesday before Ash Wednesday) has been Pancake Day since the fifteenth century. People in towns and villages eat heaps of pancakes, sing, and enjoy cock fighting, football, egg rolling, and a game called "throwing the pancake," where the winner is the one who tosses the pancake highest from the skillet to a pan. Many years ago, rural children would go from door to door, singing a begging song, trying to get a pancake. If the children were lucky, they got their cake and a cup of cider. If they received no cakes, they pelted the unhospitable home's door with rocks.

In Russia, Pancake Day is generally the Sunday before the Great Fast (Lent). Pancakes *(blini)* are part of a "little fast" preparing the system for the strict Lenten fast, when only vegetable and vegetable oils are allowed for strict Orthodox Russians. During the little fast, fish and dairy products are allowed, and people have *blini* parties with caviar, anchovies, herring, sour cream, and plenty of vodka.

Pancake Tips

1. For fluffier pancakes: Separate eggs and beat egg whites until stiff. Add whites and yolks to batter separately.

2. Let batter stand at least several minutes before using.

3. Batter, if tightly sealed, will keep for a few days in the refrigerator.

4. Cook on a nonstick surface or grease with margarine.

5. Cook on a very hot surface. The griddle is ready when a drop of water on the surface skips around and evaporates.

6. Top pancakes with your favorite syrup, fruit, or sauce. You also can roll up meat and vegetables in thin pancakes.

Apple-Cottage Cheese Pancakes

4 eggs, separated
1/8 teaspoon cream of tartar
1 cup small curd cottage cheese
1 large apple, peeled and grated
1/2 cup flour

1/4 cup whole-wheat flour
1-1/2 tablespoons honey
1 teaspoon lemon juice
1/4 teaspoon salt
1 teaspoon cinnamon

Beat egg whites and cream of tartar until stiff. Set aside. In a separate bowl, combine remaining ingredients. Fold in egg whites last. Lightly grease a skillet. Drop 1/4 cup of batter onto medium-hot skillet and cook until bubbles appear. Flip and cook other side. Top with butter, honey, or powdered sugar. Makes about 16 pancakes.

Applesauce Pancakes

1 cup flour
1-1/2 teaspoons baking powder
1/8 teaspoon salt
2 eggs, separated
1-1/2 teaspoons melted butter

1 cup applesauce
1/2 teaspoon lemon zest
1/2 teaspoon cinnamon
1/4 teaspoon vanilla extract
1 tablespoon sugar

Sift flour, baking powder, and salt into a large mixing bowl. In a separate bowl, beat egg yolks and butter; add to flour mixture. In another bowl, beat egg whites until stiff. Add remaining ingredients to the flour mixture, and fold in egg whites. Drop 1/4 cup of batter onto a hot, greased skillet. Turn pancake when bubbles appear. Serve topped with warm applesauce and cinnamon or your favorite topping. Makes 10 pancakes.

Baked Polish Pancakes with Apple Filling

Pancakes
6 tablespoons flour
1/8 teaspoon salt
1-1/4 teaspoons sugar
1-1/2 teaspoons melted butter
3 eggs, separated
3/4 cup milk
Butter for frying

Filling
2 large apples, sliced thin
3/4 teaspoon cinnamon
2-1/2 tablespoons sugar
1/3 cup melted butter for topping, divided
1/3 cup sugar for topping
1/3 cup bread crumbs for topping

Pancakes: Sift flour, salt, and sugar together. Add the melted butter and egg yolks. In a separate bowl, beat egg whites until stiff. Gradually add the milk and egg whites to the flour mixture. Butter an 8-inch frying pan and fry enough batter at a time to coat the surface of the pan. Cook until edges begin to brown; flip and cook other side. Makes about 15 pancakes.

Filling: Mix the thinly sliced apples with the cinnamon and 2-1/2 tablespoons sugar. Evenly divide the apple mixture to fill all the pancakes. Roll the pancakes and place seam side down in a buttered baking pan. Brush half of the melted butter over the pancakes. Mix the remaining butter, sugar, and bread crumbs together and sprinkle over the pancakes. Bake at 375° for 20 to 30 minutes.

Banana Pancakes

3/4 cup water
1-1/2 tablespoons brown sugar
1/2 teaspoon cinnamon

1 cup mashed bananas
1/2 cup cornmeal
1/2 teaspoon baking powder

Place all ingredients in a food processor and mix well. Drop 1/4 cup of the batter onto a greased, hot skillet. Turn pancake when edges appear firm and bubbles appear. Makes about
8 pancakes.

Basic Buttermilk Pancakes

2 cups flour
1 teaspoon baking soda
2 teaspoons baking powder
1/2 teaspoon salt

1-1/2 tablespoons sugar
1 cup buttermilk
1/4 cup margarine or butter, melted
2 eggs

Sift dry ingredients. In a separate bowl, beat the eggs and add the buttermilk and butter. Pour buttermilk mixture into flour mixture, mixing just until moist. Mixture will be lumpy but overbeating makes for tough pancakes. Drop desired amount of batter onto a hot, greased skillet. Cook until bubbles appear and begin to burst. Turn pancake and brown other side. Top with your favorite syrup, honey, powdered sugar, or fruit.

Note: See following page for delicious variations of this recipe.

Basic Buttermilk Pancake Variations

Blueberry Pancakes: Right before using the basic buttermilk pancake batter, stir in 1-1/2 cups fresh blueberries or drained, canned blueberries. If using frozen berries, thaw and drain well.

Banana Pancakes: Add 3/4 cup mashed bananas, 1 tablespoon of sugar, and 1 tablespoon cinnamon to the batter.

Whole-Wheat Pancakes: Substitute 1 cup of whole-wheat flour for 1 cup of flour.

Strawberry Pancakes: Add 1-1/2 cups fresh or well-drained canned or frozen strawberries to the batter.

Bacon Pancakes: Fry about 10 strips of bacon until crisp. Drain and chop. Add chopped bacon to the batter.

Oatmeal Pancakes: Substitute 1 cup of cooked oatmeal or any cooked cereal for about 1 cup of flour.

Onion Pancakes: Sauté 1 cup of onions and add to the batter.

Blini (Russian Pancakes)

3 cups milk, warmed, divided
1 package dry yeast
2 cups buckwheat flour, divided
4 eggs, separated

1/2 teaspoon salt
1 tablespoon sugar
2 teaspoons melted butter

Pour 1-1/2 cups of warm milk over the yeast in a bowl and stir to dissolve; add enough flour to make a thick paste. Cover the bowl; let stand in a warm place for 2-1/2 hours. Beat egg whites until stiff. In a separate bowl, beat egg yolks; add salt and sugar. Stir in 1-1/2 cups of warm milk, the butter, and the yeast mixture. Add remaining flour and egg whites. Cover and let stand for 20 minutes. Place a heaping tablespoonful of batter on a hot, greased pan. Cook about a minute or until lightly browned, then turn and brown other side. Top *blinis* with caviar and sour cream or with hard-cooked eggs, sour cream, and chives, or create your own topping. Makes about 30.

Buckwheat Pancakes

1 cup buckwheat flour	1-1/4 cups buttermilk
1 teaspoon baking powder	1/2 teaspoon baking soda
1/8 teaspoon salt	1 tablespoon cooking oil
1 egg	1 tablespoon molasses

In a mixing bowl, combine dry ingredients. In a separate bowl, combine remaining ingredients. Add to the flour mixture and beat until barely smooth. Drop 1/4 cup of batter onto hot, greased skillet. Cook until bubbles appear, then flip. Top with butter and syrup or your favorite topping. Makes 8 pancakes.

Cheesy Potato Pancakes

4 potatoes, peeled and grated
1/4 cup shredded onion
3 eggs
1 cup grated cheese

2 tablespoons flour
1/2 teaspoon salt
Dash of pepper

Combine all ingredients in a large bowl. Grease a skillet with cooking oil. Drop 1/4 cup of batter onto a medium-hot skillet. Flatten the batter with a spatula so that the pancake is about three inches in diameter. Cook until crisp and brown; flip and brown other side. Drain on paper towels. Serve plain or with warm applesauce. Makes 12 pancakes.

Chocolate Pancakes

3 cups flour
1 tablespoon baking powder
2-1/2 tablespoons sugar
1/2 teaspoon salt

1/4 cup cocoa
4 eggs
1-3/4 cups milk
1/3 cup melted butter

Combine all ingredients in order listed. Drop heaping tablespoonfuls of batter onto a hot, buttered griddle. Cook until batter bubbles and edges are firm; flip and cook the other side. Top with powdered sugar or whipped cream.

Corn Pancakes

2 cups fresh cream-style corn
1 teaspoon baking powder
1/2 teaspoon sugar
1/2 teaspoon salt
Dash of pepper

1 tablespoon melted butter
1 tablespoon cream
1 tablespoon flour
2 eggs, separated

Combine all ingredients except eggs. Beat the egg yolks and add to corn mixture. Beat the egg whites until stiff and fold into corn mixture. Drop desired amount of batter onto lightly greased hot skillet. Cook until brown; flip and cook the other side until brown.

Czech Featherweight Pancakes

1 cup dry bread crumbs
3 tablespoons melted butter
2 tablespoons brown sugar
1 teaspoon cinnamon
2 cups milk, divided

3 eggs, separated
1 cup flour
3 teaspoons baking powder
1/2 teaspoon salt

Combine bread crumbs, butter, sugar, and cinnamon and brown in a skillet, stirring constantly. Pour 1 cup of milk over the mixture and let stand until the milk is absorbed. In a mixing bowl, beat the egg yolks, add the rest of the milk, and stir in the flour, baking powder, and salt. Mix until smooth, then add crumb mixture. Beat egg whites until stiff and then fold into the batter. Drop batter onto a hot griddle and cook until edges are firm; flip and brown other side.

—George Joens, Cedar Rapids, Iowa
From The Czech Book

Danish Pancakes

4 eggs	2 cups flour
1/3 cup sugar	1-1/2 cups milk
1/2 teaspoon salt	1/2 cup beer
6 tablespoons butter, melted	Butter for frying
Grated peel from 1 lemon	

Beat together eggs, sugar, salt, and melted butter. Combine lemon peel and flour. Add flour mixture, milk, and beer alternately to the egg mixture. Mix well and refrigerate for an hour. Heat a frying pan and add some butter. Pour enough batter into the pan to create a thin layer on the bottom. While frying, shake the pan to prevent sticking. When edges are brown, flip the pancake and brown the other side. Repeat with remaining batter. Serve filled with stewed apples, jam, chopped almonds, or custard cream. Serves 6.

Dutch Baby

6 eggs
2-1/2 tablespoons sugar
3/4 cup flour
3/4 cup cream
1/2 teaspoon vanilla

1/8 teaspoon salt
1 tablespoon butter
Powdered sugar
Juice from 1/2 lemon
Sliced fresh fruit

Place eggs, sugar, flour, cream, vanilla, and salt in a blender and blend until smooth. In a 10-inch skillet, melt the butter, then pour the batter into the skillet. Bake at 425° for 15 to 20 minutes. Sprinkle with powdered sugar and lemon juice, and top with fresh fruit.

Poffertjes (Dutch Mini-Pancakes)

1 cup flour	3 eggs
4 tablespoons sugar	4 tablespoons vegetable oil
1 teaspoon salt	Butter
1 cup hot water	Powdered sugar

Mix flour, sugar, and salt. Add water, eggs, and oil. Mix well until batter is lump-free. Fry on a *poffertjes* grill or fry silver-dollar-sized pancakes in a frying pan. To serve, spread with butter and sprinkle with powdered sugar.

Note: *Poffertjes* grills may be found at kitchen specialty shops.

These pancakes are a Dutch treat served at the annual Pella, Iowa, Tulip Festival.

Finnish Pancakes with Cranberry Sauce

1 cup flour
1-1/2 cups milk
1/4 cup sugar
1/2 teaspoon cinnamon
1/4 teaspoon salt
1 tablespoon melted butter
2 eggs, separated

Thinly sliced apples for garnish

Cranberry Sauce
1 cup water, or orange juice
2-1/2 cups sugar
4 cups fresh cranberries
1/2 lemon, sliced very thin

To make pancakes: Sift flour and mix with milk until smooth. Add sugar, cinnamon, salt, and melted butter. Beat egg yolks and add to flour mixture. Beat egg whites until stiff and add to batter. Drop heaping tablespoonfuls of batter onto a greased skillet and cook until brown, then flip and brown other side. Top with apple slices and cranberry sauce. **To make sauce:** Combine all sauce ingredients in a saucepan. Bring to a boil; reduce heat and stir constantly until thickened.

Flapjacks

2 cups flour
1/2 teaspoon salt
2 teaspoons baking powder
1/2 cup cornmeal
4 tablespoons bacon drippings
Water

Sift flour, salt, and baking powder together. Stir in cornmeal and bacon drippings. Add enough water to make batter the desired consistency. More water makes a thinner pancake. Use enough batter to cover the bottom of a 10-inch greased skillet. Brown the flapjack; flip and brown other side. Stack the flapjacks with butter and maple syrup between each layer. Cut into wedges and serve.

German Baked Apple Pancake

4 egg whites
1/3 cup sugar, divided
1 cup flour
1/8 teaspoon salt
1 cup beer, room temperature
2 egg yolks
2 teaspoons cinnamon

1/4 cup brown sugar
2 large green apples, peeled, cored,
    and sliced
1/2 lemon
3 tablespoons butter
1 tablespoon vegetable oil

Beat egg whites and 1 teaspoon sugar until stiff. In another bowl, sift together 2 teaspoons sugar, the flour, and salt. Gradually beat in beer and egg yolks. Fold in egg whites. Combine the remaining sugar, cinnamon, and brown sugar, reserving 2 teaspoons of the mixture for serving. Toss apple slices with the lemon juice and mix in the cinnamon-sugar. Heat the butter and oil in a 9-inch skillet or pan. Pour in half the batter, cover with the apples, and pour in the rest of the batter. Bake at 350° for an hour or until pancake is puffy and golden. Sprinkle with remaining cinnamon and sugar; cut into wedges and serve.

"I ate pancakes similar to these at a restaurant once and loved them so much I had to make them myself. I searched for years before I found this recipe, and it was worth it. This pancake is great! I heard of one person who regularly traveled to a restaurant an hour away to get his fill of this delicious pancake," says Penfield editor Maureen Patterson. *"I substitute water for the beer. This pancake can be either a main dish or a dessert."*

Gingerbread Pancakes

2-1/2 cups cake flour
1-1/2 teaspoons baking soda
1 teaspoon ground ginger
1-1/2 teaspoons cinnamon
1/8 teaspoon ground cloves
1/8 teaspoon salt

1-1/4 cups molasses
1/2 cup coffee, cooled
1/4 cup water
1 egg, beaten
1/2 cup melted butter

Sift dry ingredients together into a mixing bowl. In a separate bowl, mix remaining ingredients. Slowly add the wet ingredients to the dry, mixing well. Drop desired amount of batter onto a lightly greased, low-heat skillet. Cook until bubbles appear, then flip and cook other side. Top with whipped cream, powdered sugar, or lemon applesauce (page 112).

Greek Pancakes with Honey Syrup

Pancakes
1-3/4 cups flour
1/8 teaspoon salt
1 teaspoon baking powder
1 tablespoon sugar
1-1/2 cups milk
3 eggs
Butter for frying

Syrup

1 cup honey
3/4 teaspoon cinnamon
1 teaspoon sesame seeds

To make syrup: Bring honey to a boil and remove from heat. Add cinnamon and sesame seeds and serve warm.

To make pancakes: Combine dry ingredients. In a large bowl, mix milk and eggs. Gradually add the dry ingredients to the egg mixture, beating until smooth. Pour 1/4 cup of batter onto a hot skillet greased with 1 teaspoon butter. Cook pancake until it bubbles, then flip and cook other side. Add butter as needed to the skillet until all the pancakes are cooked. Makes about 15 pancakes.

Hearty Molasses Hotcakes

3 cups flour
2 tablespoons baking powder
1/2 teaspoon salt
1/2 teaspoon baking soda
1-1/2 cups cornmeal

2 tablespoons molasses
2 cups water
5 eggs
2 cups buttermilk
1/3 cup melted butter

Sift flour, baking powder, salt, and soda and set aside. Mix the cornmeal and the molasses. Bring the water to a boil and pour over the cornmeal mixture, stirring until thick and cool. Add the dry ingredients, then the eggs, buttermilk, and melted butter. Drop 1/2 cup of batter onto a hot, lightly greased skillet. Cook until brown; flip and brown other side. Serve with your favorite topping.

Hungarian Pancakes

1 cup milk
3/4 teaspoon sugar
1/8 teaspoon salt
3 eggs

1-1/4 cups flour
1 cup carbonated water
Butter for frying

Combine milk, sugar, salt, eggs, and flour and let batter rest for about an hour. Stir in carbonated water right before cooking pancakes. Butter an 8-inch frying pan and pour in enough batter to cover the bottom of the pan. When the pancake bubbles, flip it and brown the other side. Add butter before cooking each pancake. Makes about 12 pancakes.

Icelandic Pancakes

2 eggs
1/3 cup sugar
1/4 teaspoon salt
1/2 teaspoon cinnamon
1/2 teaspoon baking soda

1 teaspoon baking powder
1-1/2 cups flour
1/2 teaspoon vanilla
1/2 cup sour cream
2 cups milk

Beat all ingredients together until smooth. Batter will be thin. Pour a little batter into a hot skillet and spread to form a thin layer across the bottom. When brown, flip the pancake and brown the other side. Repeat with remaining batter. Serve sprinkled with additional sugar. Serves 4.

Indian Fried Bread

6 to 8 cups flour, divided
1 tablespoon baking powder
1 teaspoon sugar

1/2 teaspoon salt
1-1/2 cups lukewarm water
Shortening for frying

Pour 6 cups flour into a large bowl. Make a well in the middle of the flour. Dissolve baking powder, sugar, and salt in the water. Pour mixture into the well. Stir the liquid (counterclockwise only) in the well and the liquid will pick up the right amount of flour. Stir until the mixture thickens to a point where it will no longer stir readily and the dough rolls around. On a lightly floured surface, knead the dough with floured hands, adding flour until the dough is no longer sticky. Return dough to bowl and set aside for 30 to 60 minutes before frying.

continued

Indian Fried Bread *continued*

In a skillet or deep fryer, heat 2 to 3 inches of shortening until hot, about 375°; do not overheat. Cut off a handful of the dough and place it on a floured board and pat into a patty 6 to 8 inches in diameter and 1/3-inch thick. Cut the patty into 6 pieces. Slit each of the pieces through the middle. Place the pieces gently into the hot oil and fry until brown on each side. Remove from the oil and drain on absorbent paper. Repeat with remaining dough. Serve warm plain or rolled in cinnamon and sugar. Also great with jam and butter.

— *Lac du Flambeau Wisconsin Chamber of Commerce*

Jewish Potato *Latkes*

6 potatoes, peeled and grated	Dash of pepper
2 eggs	1 small onion, grated
2 tablespoons flour	1/4 teaspoon baking powder
1/2 teaspoon salt	Oil for frying

Using paper towels, squeeze the moisture from the grated potatoes. Add all the ingredients together and mix well. Pour 1/4 inch of oil into a skillet and heat. Drop batter by heaping tablespoonfuls onto the hot skillet. Fry pancakes until edges brown; flip and fry other side. Turn only once or the pancakes will get soggy. Serve plain or with applesauce and sour cream.

Johnnycakes

1-1/4 cups boiling water 1 teaspoon salt
1 cup stone-ground white cornmeal

Bring water to a boil; remove from heat. Add cornmeal and salt, stirring until smooth. Drop tablespoonfuls of batter onto a greased, hot skillet and fry one side for about 6 minutes. Flip and cook the other side about 5 minutes or until done. Top with syrup, jam, honey, or butter. Makes about 8 Johnnycakes.

Chinese Mandarin Pancakes

1-1/2 cups flour
1/2 teaspoon sesame oil
1/4 teaspoon salt

3/4 cup water, boiling
1 tablespoon sesame oil for brushing

Place flour, 1/2 teaspoon oil, and salt in a mixing bowl. Gradually add boiling water; mix with a spoon until a soft dough forms. On a lightly floured surface, knead the dough until smooth. Add more flour to the dough if it is sticky. Cover and let rest for 15 minutes. Divide dough into 16 walnut-sized balls, then flatten each ball on a floured surface. Brush 8 of the pancakes with oil, then top each oiled pancake with an unoiled one. With a rolling pin, flatten the 8 pancakes into 5-inch circles, rolling both sides. Place 1 stacked pancake in an ungreased, medium-hot, 8-inch skillet. Cook until top puffs and bubbles, then turn and cook the other side, about 1 minute on each side. Separate into 16 thin pancakes before serving. Great wrapped around stir-fried meats and vegetables.

Matzo Meal Pancakes

3 eggs, separated
1/2 tablespoon sugar
1/2 cup matzo meal

1/4 teaspoon salt
1/2 cup water

Mix the egg yolks and sugar until light. In a separate bowl, blend matzo meal with salt and water. Add to egg yolk mixture. Beat egg whites until stiff; fold into matzo mixture. Drop by heaping tablespoonfuls onto a well-greased, hot skillet and fry until brown. Flip and fry other side. Serve with sour cream, applesauce, or jam.

Norwegian Cottage Cheese Pancakes

1 cup cottage cheese
6 eggs
1/8 teaspoon salt

1/3 cup rye flour
1/3 cup melted butter

Place all ingredients in a blender and blend until smooth. Drop heaping table-spoonfuls of batter onto a hot, buttered griddle. Cook until edges are firm and bubbles appear; flip and brown other side. Serve topped with applesauce, jam, or your favorite topping.

Panqueque de Alejandro (Chilean Pancakes)

1 egg
1-1/2 cups whole milk

1 cup flour

Lightly beat the egg; add the milk and flour. Drop about 1/4 cup of batter into a nonstick or lightly greased skillet. Fry until set; flip and fry other side. Top *panqueques* with butter and powdered sugar or with jam. You can roll them up or fold them into triangles for serving. Makes 6 to 8 very thin pancakes.

Note: In Chile these pancakes are served topped with *manjar*—boiled condensed milk. *Manjar* is an extremely popular topping and filling used for many sweets in Chile.

—José Alejandro Cid
Santiago, Chile

Peanut Butter Pancakes

1/3 cup peanut butter
1/3 cup melted butter
2 eggs
1/2 teaspoon sugar

1/8 teaspoon salt
1-1/4 teaspoons baking powder
1-1/4 cups milk
1-1/4 cups flour

In a large mixing bowl, mix peanut butter, melted butter, and eggs. Add the rest of the ingredients. Let batter stand, refrigerated, a few hours before using. Drop desired amount of batter on a hot, greased skillet and cook until brown. Flip and brown the other side. Serve with butter and syrup or with jam.

Popover Pancake

3 tablespoons butter
2 eggs
1/2 cup milk

1/2 cup flour
1/2 teaspoon cinnamon

Melt margarine in an 8-inch skillet in an oven. Place remaining ingredients in a blender and blend until smooth. Pour batter into buttered skillet and bake at 400° until the edges are golden and pancake is puffed.

Puffy Danish Pancake

1/4 cup butter
3/4 cup milk

3/4 cup flour
3 eggs

Melt butter in an iron skillet in a 425° oven. Combine the remaining ingredients in a blender. Pour the well-blended mixture into the skillet with butter, and bake for 12 to 15 minutes. Serve topped with fresh fruit or powdered sugar.

Pumpkin Pancakes

1 egg	3/4 cup milk
1 teaspoon baking powder	3/4 teaspoon cinnamon
2-1/2 tablespoons brown sugar	1/4 teaspoon ground cloves
1 cup canned pumpkin	1/8 teaspoon nutmeg
1/4 cup whole-wheat flour	1 cup chopped walnuts or pecans

Place all ingredients except nuts in a blender and mix well. Drop, 1/4 cup at a time, onto a greased, hot pan. Flip pancake when bubbles appear and edges look firm. Top pancakes with nuts and maple syrup or with sour cream. Makes about 8 pancakes.

Raisin Buttermilk Pancakes

1 cup raisins
1 teaspoon cinnamon
1/4 cup sugar, divided
3 eggs, separated
1-3/4 cups buttermilk

1 teaspoon baking soda
3 tablespoons margarine, melted
1-1/2 cups flour
1 teaspoon baking powder
1/2 teaspoon salt

Soak raisins in hot water until plump, then drain and dry on paper towels. Mix cinnamon and 2 tablespoons of sugar and add the raisins. In a separate bowl, beat egg whites until soft peaks form; add remaining sugar and beat until stiff. In another bowl, beat egg yolks until creamy and stir in buttermilk, soda, and margarine. Sift the flour, baking powder, and salt into the buttermilk mixture. Fold in egg whites and raisins. Drop 1/4 cup of batter on a hot, lightly greased skillet. Cook until bubbles appear; flip and cook other side. Makes about 16 pancakes.

Shrovetide Pancakes

6 eggs, separated
1-1/2 cups flour, sifted
1/2 teaspoon salt

1-1/4 teaspoons grated lemon zest
1-1/2 cups milk

Beat egg whites until stiff; set aside. Beat egg yolks and set aside. Mix flour, salt, and lemon zest; add egg yolks and milk. Fold in egg whites. Pour enough batter on a greased, hot skillet to make a thin, 5-inch pancake. Cook until light brown and turn. Spread pancakes with jelly or sprinkle with sugar and roll up. Makes about 18 pancakes.

Spicy Apple Pancakes with Cider Sauce

Pancakes
1 cup biscuit mix
1/4 teaspoon cinnamon
2/3 cup milk
1 egg
1 apple, grated

Cider Sauce
1/2 cup sugar
1 tablespoon cornstarch
1/8 teaspoon cinnamon
1/8 teaspoon nutmeg
1 cup apple cider
1 tablespoon lemon juice
2 tablespoons butter

Pancakes: Beat biscuit mix, cinnamon, milk, and egg together until smooth. Stir in the grated apple. Pour 1/4 cup of batter onto lightly greased 325° griddle. Fry until bubbles appear and edges are cooked; flip and brown other side. Place in 300° oven until ready to serve. Makes about a dozen pancakes.

continued

Spicy Apple Pancakes with Cider Sauce *continued*

Cider Sauce: In a saucepan, mix sugar, cornstarch, cinnamon, and nutmeg. Stir in apple cider and lemon juice. Cook, stirring constantly, until mixture thickens and boils. Boil, stirring constantly, for 1 minute. Remove from heat and stir in butter. Serve warm over pancakes.

—Ida M. Sessler
Jackson Street Inn Bed and Breakfast
Janesville, Wisconsin

Spinach Pancakes

1/2 cup plain yogurt
3/4 cup whole-wheat flour
1/2 teaspoon baking powder

1/2 cup water
1 cup chopped fresh spinach
1 egg

Combine all ingredients in a bowl. Drop 1/4 cup of batter onto greased, hot skillet. Cook about a minute on each side. For a delicious lunch or dinner, try rolling up pieces of meat, vegetables, or cheese in this pancake. Makes about 8 pancakes.

- 51 -

Swedish Oven Pancake

1 cup milk
2/3 cup flour
2 tablespoons sugar
1/2 teaspoon salt

2 eggs
1/2 teaspoon ground cardamom
1/4 cup butter

Beat all ingredients except butter until smooth. Place butter in a 9-inch pan and put into a 400° oven until the butter melts. Pour batter into the pan with butter and bake for 35 minutes or until deep brown and puffy. Serves 2.

Swedish Pancakes

2 egg yolks
4 eggs
2-1/4 cups milk

1/4 cup sugar
1-1/2 cups flour
1/2 cup butter, melted

Mix all ingredients together. Set aside for at least half an hour or up to overnight in the refrigerator. On a hot griddle spread about 1/4 cup of batter out thinly. Fry on both sides until golden brown. Repeat with remaining batter. Serve with lingonberries, jam, or syrup. Serves 3.

—Glen and Virginia Arnold
The Swedish Mill, Kingsburg, California
From Splendid Swedish Recipes

Wisconsin-Swiss Pancakes

2 cups buttermilk baking mix
1-1/2 cups milk
1/2 cup sour cream
1 egg

1/4 teaspoon nutmeg
6 ounces shredded Wisconsin Swiss
  Cheese
Sautéed apple slices (optional)

In a large mixing bowl, combine all ingredients except cheese and apple slices. Blend at low speed just until ingredients are combined. Stir in cheese. Allow batter to stand while heating griddle to about 375°. Use a scant 1/4 cup batter for each pancake. Pour onto a lightly greased griddle. Cook until bubbles break on the surface and edges are cooked; turn and cook other side until golden. Serve warm with sautéed apple slices. Makes about 20 pancakes.

—*Wisconsin Milk Marketing Board*
Madison, Wisconsin

Waffles

Waffles

It is believed that waffles evolved out of Holy Bread—small, crisp wafers offered at communion. Whatever the origin, waffles date at least to the twelfth century, when the French *gaufre* was sold on the streets of Paris. Author Geoffrey Chaucer mentioned them in his fourteenth-century *Canterbury Tales*. These were baked by street vendors who held long-handled irons over a fire to produce crispy treats sold with a sweet sauce.

The word waffle comes from the Dutch word *wafel*. When Thomas Jefferson was in Holland in 1789, he was so impressed with his first taste of waffles that he bought a pair of waffle irons and tongs for one and a third Dutch florins, according to *The Williamsburg Cookbook*. When the Dutch emigrated to New York, it was their custom to give a new bride a waffle iron decorated with her initials and the date of the wedding. Today, waffles are made of batter thicker than pancake batter and are usually made in an electric waffle iron that bakes each waffle to crispy perfection.

Waffle Tips

1. Follow manufacturer's directions for your waffle iron.
2. Before using your iron for the first time, season it with unsalted fat.
3. Heat the iron completely before adding the batter. A drop of water sprinkled on the surface will skip around and evaporate when the waffle iron is ready.
4. Pour the batter into the center of the iron until it spreads to cover the entire surface.
5. Close the iron and bake until it quits steaming.
6. Remove the waffle with a spatula or fork.
7. Batter keeps in the refrigerator for about two days when tightly sealed.
8. Top waffles with fruits, syrups, jam, powdered sugar, ice cream, or, for lunch or dinner, with creamy meat and seafood sauces.

Bacon and Cheese Waffles

1-1/2 cups flour
1-1/2 cups milk
1/4 cup butter or margarine, melted
2 eggs, slightly beaten
1 tablespoon baking powder

1/8 teaspoon salt
6 to 8 slices of bacon,
    cooked and crumbled
2/3 cup grated Cheddar cheese

Combine all ingredients except the bacon and cheese. Stir until smooth. Add the bacon and cheese and stir gently. Cook in a waffle iron. Top with butter and syrup. Makes 5 waffles.

Basic Waffles

See following page for delicious variations.

2 cups flour
1 tablespoon baking powder
1/2 teaspoon baking soda
1/2 teaspoon salt

1-1/2 cups buttermilk
3 eggs
1/2 cup melted butter or margarine

Sift together the dry ingredients. Add the buttermilk, eggs, and melted butter, mixing until there are no more lumps. Bake in a waffle iron.

Note: You may substitute an equal amount of yogurt, sour milk, cream, or sour cream for the buttermilk.

Basic Waffle Variations

Apple Waffles: Stir 2 cups peeled, diced apples into waffle batter.

Banana Waffles: Stir 1-1/2 cups thinly sliced bananas into waffle batter.

Cocoa Waffles: Substitute 3 tablespoons of cocoa for 3 tablespoons of flour.

Cornmeal Waffles: Substitute 1/2 cup of the flour with cornmeal.

Fruit Waffles: Stir 1 cup drained berries or other thinly sliced fruit into batter.

Fudge Waffles: Add 1/3 cup cocoa, 1 teaspoon vanilla, and 1/3 cup sugar.

Nut Waffles: Stir 1 cup finely chopped nuts into the batter.

Orange Waffles: Use 1/2 cup orange juice in place of 1/2 cup of the milk and add 1 tablespoon grated orange rind to the batter.

Whole Grain Waffles: Substitute 1/2 cup of the flour with rye meal, whole-wheat flour, or graham flour.

Belgian Waffles

1-1/2 cups flour	3 eggs, separated
2 teaspoons baking powder	3/4 cup buttermilk
1/2 teaspoon baking soda	3/4 cup sour cream
1/8 teaspoon salt	1/4 cup shortening, melted
2 tablespoons sugar	1/4 cup butter, melted

Combine dry ingredients. In a separate bowl, beat egg yolks, buttermilk, and sour cream together. Add the buttermilk mixture, the melted, cooled shortening, and butter gradually to the flour mixture. Stir until smooth. Beat egg whites until stiff and fold into batter. Cook in a waffle iron. Serve with a fruit topping or other favorite topping. Makes 10 waffles.

Brownie Waffle Cookies

1/3 cup butter
1 ounce unsweetened chocolate
1 egg
1/2 cup sugar
2 tablespoons milk

1/2 teaspoon vanilla
3/4 cup flour
1/2 teaspoon baking powder
1 cup finely chopped nuts, divided

Melt butter and chocolate over low heat; cool. Combine egg, sugar, milk, and vanilla; add to the chocolate mixture. In a separate bowl, combine flour and baking powder and add to the chocolate mixture. Add 2/3 cup of the nuts. Preheat waffle iron to medium. Drop batter by level tablespoonfuls onto the iron about 3 inches apart. Sprinkle with the remaining nuts. Close iron and bake about 3 minutes or until done. Cool on wire racks. Makes 2 dozen.

Cheesy Waffles

3 eggs, separated
2 cups milk
2 cups grated American cheese
2 cups flour

1-1/2 tablespoons sugar
1/2 teaspoon salt
2 teaspoons baking powder
1/2 cup butter, melted

Beat egg yolks until light and fluffy; mix in milk and cheese. Sift dry ingredients together and add to the milk mixture. Stir until blended; add the melted butter. Beat the egg whites until stiff and add to the batter. Bake in a hot waffle iron. Makes about 8 waffles.

Coconut Waffles

1-1/2 cups flour	3 eggs, separated
1-1/2 teaspoons baking powder	1-1/2 cups milk
1/8 teaspoon salt	3 tablespoons butter, melted
1 tablespoon sugar	1 cup flaked coconut, divided

Sift together the dry ingredients. In a separate bowl, beat the egg yolks and milk, then add to the flour mixture. Stir in the melted butter and 3/4 cup of the coconut. In a separate bowl, beat the egg whites until stiff. Fold into the batter. Cook in a medium-hot waffle iron. Sprinkle with remaining grated coconut before serving. Top with melted butter, coconut syrup, or butterscotch sauce (page 117).

Dutch Waffles

4 eggs, separated
2 cups milk
3 cups flour, sifted
5 teaspoons baking powder

1 teaspoon salt
2 teaspoons sugar
2/3 cup melted butter or margarine

Beat egg yolks; add milk, sifted dry ingredients, and melted butter. Beat egg whites until stiff and fold into batter. Cook in a waffle iron until edges are lightly browned.

Finnish Waffles

3 eggs
3 cups heavy cream, whipped
1-1/2 cups flour

1/8 teaspoon salt
2-1/2 tablespoons sugar
1/4 cup melted butter

Beat eggs until very light and fluffy. Fold in the whipped cream, flour, salt, sugar, and melted butter. Cook in a waffle iron until golden. Makes 12 eight-inch waffles.

French *Gaufres*

1 cup sugar	1-1/2 cups flour
3/4 cup sweet butter	1/3 cup milk
4 eggs, separated	3/4 teaspoon vanilla

Cream sugar and butter until very light; add egg yolks 1 at a time. Beat well. Sift flour into the mixture; add milk and vanilla and beat until smooth. In a separate bowl, beat egg whites until stiff; add to batter. Bake in a hot waffle iron. Serve with whipped cream, powdered sugar, or ice cream.

Gingerbread Waffles

2 cups flour
2 teaspoons baking powder
1/2 teaspoon baking soda
2-1/2 teaspoons cinnamon
1 teaspoon ginger

1/8 teaspoon salt
1/3 cup butter or margarine
1 cup molasses
2 eggs, separated
1/2 cup buttermilk

Sift together dry ingredients and set aside. Beat butter, molasses, and egg yolks until smooth. Add the dry ingredients to the butter mixture alternately with the buttermilk. In a separate bowl, beat the egg whites until stiff; fold into the batter. Bake in a hot waffle iron. Serve with apple cinnamon sauce (page 112), whipped cream, or melted butter and powdered sugar.

Overnight Yeast Waffles

1 package dry yeast
1/4 cup warm water
1-1/4 cups milk
2 cups flour

1/8 teaspoon salt
1 egg
3 tablespoons butter or margarine, melted

Dissolve the yeast in the water. Scald milk and cool to lukewarm; add to yeast. Sift flour and salt into the yeast mixture; stir. Cover and let stand overnight in a warm place free of drafts. Stir in the rest of the ingredients in the morning. Bake in a hot waffle iron. Makes about 8 waffles.

Peach Waffles

2 cups flour
1 tablespoon baking powder
1/8 teaspoon salt
1/3 cup shortening
1/2 cup sugar

2 eggs
1 cup milk
1-1/2 cups peeled, diced peaches
1 tablespoon lemon juice
1/2 teaspoon vanilla

Combine dry ingredients and set aside. Beat shortening, sugar, and eggs thoroughly. To the shortening mixture, add the dry ingredients alternately with the milk. Add remaining ingredients. Bake in a waffle iron and serve with additional sliced, fresh peaches, and/or whipped cream. Makes 16 four-inch waffles.

Potato Waffles

3 eggs
1 cup flour
2 teaspoons baking powder
1/8 teaspoon salt

1 cup milk
1 tablespoon shortening, melted
2 cups cold mashed potatoes

Beat eggs until light and fluffy. Sift the dry ingredients; add to the eggs. Stir in the milk, melted shortening, and potatoes. Bake in a hot waffle iron. Serve with butter and warm syrup. Makes 4 waffles.

Raisin Oatmeal Waffles

1-1/2 cups flour
1 tablespoon baking powder
1/8 teaspoon salt
1 tablespoon sugar
1/2 cup quick-cooking oats, uncooked

1 teaspoon ground cinnamon
2 eggs, slightly beaten
1-1/2 cups milk
1/4 cup butter, melted
1/4 cup raisins, chopped

Combine the dry ingredients and mix well. In a separate bowl, combine the eggs, milk, and butter. Gradually add the milk mixture to the flour mixture, stirring until no lumps remain. Stir in the chopped raisins. Bake in a waffle iron. Serve with butter and syrup or a fruit syrup. Makes 12 four-inch waffles.

Rice Flour Waffles

3 eggs, separated
1-3/4 cups milk
1/4 cup cooking oil
1-3/4 cups rice flour

2 tablespoons brown sugar
3 teaspoons baking powder
1/2 teaspoon salt

Beat egg yolks until thick, then add milk and oil. In a separate bowl, combine flour, sugar, baking powder, and salt. Add the egg yolk mixture to the dry ingredients and beat until smooth. Beat egg whites until stiff, then fold into batter. Cook in a waffle iron. Top with fruit sauce, butter and syrup, or your favorite topping. Makes 12 four-inch waffles.

Rice Waffles

4 cups biscuit mix
3-1/3 cups milk
2 eggs

4 tablespoons vegetable oil
2 cups cooked rice

Combine all ingredients in order listed, until smooth. Cook in a hot waffle iron. Serve with butter and warm syrup. Makes 10 waffles.

Rich Waffles

These waffles are great for dessert.

1-1/2 cups sifted cake flour
3 teaspoons baking powder
1/8 teaspoon salt
1 teaspoon sugar

3 eggs, separated
1 cup heavy cream
1/4 cup melted butter or margarine

Sift together dry ingredients. In a separate bowl, combine egg yolks, cream, and melted butter, mixing well; add to the flour mixture. In another bowl, beat egg whites until stiff; add to the batter. Cook in a hot waffle iron. Makes 4 waffles.

Southern Grits Waffles

1 cup hominy grits, cooked
1 egg, beaten
1 cup rice flour
1/3 cup whole-wheat flour

1/8 teaspoon salt
1 cup milk
1/3 cup water
1 tablespoon butter, melted

Mix grits and eggs together. In a separate bowl, mix the dry ingredients; add the milk and water and then the grits mixture. Add the melted butter last. Cook in a hot waffle iron. Serve with plenty of butter and warm syrup. Makes about 12 waffles.

Swedish Waffles

1-1/3 cups whipping cream, whipped   1/3 cup ice cold water (or snow)
1 cup flour   2 tablespoons butter, melted

Fold whipped cream into the flour. Add other ingredients. Let set for an hour. Bake in a waffle iron until brown. This is a crisp waffle. Cool and serve with powdered sugar or lingonberries.

Note: Sour cream can be substituted for a third of the amount of whipping cream.

Sweet Potato Waffles

2 cups pastry flour
4 teaspoons baking powder
1/8 teaspoon salt
3/4 tablespoon sugar
1/2 teaspoon cinnamon

2 eggs, separated
1 cup cooked, mashed sweet potatoes
1-1/2 cups milk
1/2 cup melted butter or margarine

In a mixing bowl, add the dry ingredients, egg yolks, sweet potatoes, milk, and butter and mix well. In a separate bowl, beat egg whites until stiff; fold into the batter. Cook in a waffle iron and serve plain or with butter and syrup.

Whole-Wheat Waffles

1-1/2 cups flour
1/2 cup whole-wheat flour
2 teaspoons baking powder
1-1/2 teaspoons baking soda
3/4 teaspoon cinnamon

1/8 teaspoon salt
1-1/3 cups buttermilk
1-1/3 cups apple juice
1 tablespoon honey
4 egg whites

Combine dry ingredients. Add the buttermilk, juice, and honey. In a separate bowl, beat the egg whites until stiff; add to batter. Cook in a waffle iron until done. Serve with butter and maple syrup or with apple cinnamon sauce (page 112). Makes 6 waffles.

Crêpes and Blintzes

How to Make Crêpes

Crêpe is a French word meaning pancake. Although the word is French, the food is international. Jews have blintzes, Mexicans have *enchiladas*, the Chinese have egg roll, Greeks have *kreps*, Italians have *cannelloni*, Hungarians have *palacsinta*, Russians the *blini*, and Scandinavians enjoy *plättar*.

Crêpes can be made in a greased 6-, 7-, or 9-inch skillet or in special crêpe pans. If using a crêpe maker, follow the manufacturer's directions since some require the crêpe to be cooked on both sides, and others browned on just one side. If using a skillet, grease it with oil or butter if it is not a nonstick pan. Heat the skillet, then pour 2 or 3 tablespoons of batter into the skillet, tilting the skillet quickly so that the batter covers the bottom of the pan before it sets. Return the skillet to medium-high heat and cook until the bottom is brown, about 1 minute. Turn the crêpe carefully with a spatula and cook the other side for about 30 seconds. If the crêpe tears, patch it with a little batter and continue cooking.

Crêpe Tips

1. Spread crêpes with butter and powdered sugar or with jam or honey. Fill crêpes with fruit, ice cream, meats, cheeses, vegetables, or fish.

2. Store cooked crêpes in foil or a plastic bag in the refrigerator for up to 5 days. Reheat by briefly cooking in a greased pan or by filling the crêpe and putting it in the oven.

3. Freeze unfilled crêpes by stacking them with two sheets of waxed paper between each crêpe. Put the stacked crêpes in a plastic freezer bag and freeze for up to 6 months. Frozen crêpes break easily, so staple paper plates around the crêpes in the freezer bag for protection, or put into a plastic container. Thaw at room temperature or remove waxed paper, wrap crêpes in foil, and warm in oven.

4. Freeze filled crêpes by placing them on a greased baking sheet in the freezer until frozen. Then place crêpes in a plastic bag and freeze for up to 2 months.

How to Fold Crêpes

1. Serve flat with toppings spread on top.
2. Stack up several crêpes with a filling spread between each layer. Cut in wedges.
3. Spread filling along center of crêpe. Fold one side over to the filling, then fold over the other side, so the ends overlap the filling.
4. Place filling on half of the crêpe, and fold the other side over so the crêpe looks like a taco.
5. Spread filling on crêpe, then fold in half, then in half again to form a triangle.
6. Spread filling on crêpe, leave a 1/4-inch border, and roll crêpe like a jelly roll.
7. Fold into quarters and open one pocket; spoon in filling.
8. To fold blintzes, spoon filling into the center of crêpe. Fold both sides over the filling, then fold over the bottom and top, forming a tight pocket.

Basic Crêpe Batter

4 eggs
2-1/4 cups milk
1/4 cup melted butter

1/8 teaspoon salt
2 cups flour

Combine all ingredients in a blender and blend well. Scrape sides and blend again for 10 seconds. You also may combine all ingredients in a mixing bowl with a whisk or mixer. Makes about 32 crêpes.

Blueberry Blintzes

Batter
1 cup flour
1 cup milk
1/8 teaspoon salt
2 eggs
Butter for frying

Filling
1-1/2 cups cottage cheese
1 egg, beaten
1 tablespoon sugar
1 tablespoon honey
1 teaspoon cinnamon
1/8 teaspoon salt
1-1/4 cups blueberries (fresh or frozen,
  thawed and drained), divided

To make batter: Place all batter ingredients in a blender and mix until smooth. Melt butter in an 8-inch crêpe pan and add about 3 tablespoons of batter, enough

continued

Blueberry Blintzes *continued*

to coat the bottom. Cook one side only until golden brown. Makes 10 blintzes.

To make filling: Strain and discard liquid from cottage cheese. Add remaining ingredients and 1 cup of the blueberries, making sure the berries are well-drained.

To assemble: Place a heaping tablespoon of mixture on each blintz, folding like an envelope (see page 83). Sauté blintzes in butter until golden brown. Top with the remaining blueberries and cinnamon and sugar, or with vanilla yogurt or sour cream.

Cheese Blintzes

Batter
1/2 cup flour
1/8 teaspoon salt
2 eggs, beaten
2/3 cup milk
1 tablespoon melted butter

Filling
1/2 pound dry cottage cheese
2 egg yolks
1/2 teaspoon cinnamon
2 tablespoons sugar
Dash of salt (optional)
Butter for frying

Batter: Sift flour and salt together; add rest of batter ingredients and mix until smooth. Drop about 3 tablespoons of the batter onto a hot 6-inch skillet. Tilt pan to cover bottom. Cook one side only until it is brown.

continued

Cheese Blintzes *continued*

Filling: Put cottage cheese through a sieve; discard liquid. Add remaining ingredients to the cottage cheese and mix well.

Assembly: Place a tablespoon of filling in the center of each blintz on the brown side. Fold like an envelope (see page 83). Fry in butter until both sides are golden brown. You also can bake blintzes in a greased baking pan. Brush the tops with melted butter and sprinkle blintzes with cinnamon and sugar.

Chocolate Crêpes

3 eggs
1-1/4 cups buttermilk
2 tablespoons cocoa

1 cup flour
2 tablespoons sugar
2 tablespoons melted butter

Combine all ingredients in a blender and blend well. Scrape sides and blend again for 10 seconds. You may also combine all ingredients in a mixing bowl with a whisk or mixer. Makes about 20 crêpes.

Finnish Crêpes

1 cup buttermilk
1/2 teaspoon salt
1 teaspoon sugar

2 eggs
2 tablespoons melted butter
1 cup flour

Place all ingredients in a blender and mix until smooth. Drop about 2 or 3 tablespoonfuls of batter into a hot, greased skillet or a Scandinavian pancake pan. Cook both sides until golden. Makes about 20.

Finnish Oatmeal Crêpes

1 cup oat flour*
1/2 cup milk
2 eggs

1/2 cup heavy cream
1/8 teaspoon salt
Butter for frying

Combine all ingredients in a blender and mix until smooth. Drop about 2 tablespoons of batter onto a hot, greased skillet, making the crêpe about 3 inches wide. Cook one side only until set, then roll up, brown side on the outside. Serve with cinnamon, sugar, and cream.

*To make 1 cup of oat flour, place 1-1/4 cups oats in a food processor or blender and blend until powdery like flour.

French Soufflé Crêpes

6 eggs, separated
1-1/2 cups light cream
3/4 cup flour

1/8 teaspoon salt
1/2 teaspoon baking powder

Beat egg whites until stiff but not dry; set aside. Beat egg yolks until light; stir in cream. Sift remaining ingredients into the egg yolks and cream. Mix well. Fold in egg whites. Pour 1/2 cup batter into an 8-inch buttered skillet; cook both sides until golden. Makes about 12 crêpes.

Herb Crêpes

3/4 teaspoon dried, crushed
    tarragon leaves
1 tablespoon finely chopped parsley
1-1/2 tablespoons finely chopped
    chives

1/4 cup melted butter
3 eggs
2 cups flour
1 cup milk
1 cup chicken bouillon

Combine all ingredients in a blender and blend well. Scrape sides and blend again for 10 seconds. You may also combine all ingredients in a mixing bowl with a whisk or mixer. Makes about 25 crêpes.

Lemon Crêpes

2 eggs
Dash of salt
1 cup flour
1-1/2 cups milk
2 tablespoons sugar
1 tablespoon cooking oil
1-1/4 teaspoons grated lemon zest

Place all ingredients in a blender and mix until smooth. Drop about 2 tablespoonfuls of batter onto a hot, greased 6-inch skillet, tilting pan until batter covers the bottom. Cook one side only until brown.

Parmesan Cheese Crêpes

1/4 cup grated Parmesan cheese
2 eggs
1-1/2 cups milk
1 cup flour
Vegetable oil for frying

Put all ingredients, except oil, in a blender and mix until smooth. Drop 2 tablespoonfuls of batter onto a hot, oiled 6-inch skillet, tilting the pan so the batter covers the bottom. Cook one side only until brown. Makes about 18 crêpes.

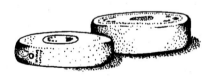

Potato Blintzes

Batter
1/2 cup milk
3/4 teaspoon sugar
1/8 teaspoon salt
1/2 cup flour
1 egg

Filling
2 medium-sized onions, finely chopped
Butter for frying
3 potatoes, cooked and mashed
1 egg
Dash of salt and pepper

Batter: Combine all batter ingredients until smooth. Cook about 3 tablespoonfuls of batter in a skillet or in a crêpe maker. Cook until the blintz is light brown on one side only, then remove from skillet. Makes 6 blintzes. **Filling:** Sauté onions in butter until brown; add to mashed potatoes. Add egg, salt, and pepper and mix until light and fluffy. Divide filling evenly among the blintzes, placing filling in the center. Fold into a pocket (see page 83). Fry each blintz in butter until golden. Serve with sour cream.

Potato Crêpes

3 eggs
3/4 cup milk
1/8 teaspoon salt
Dash of pepper

Dash of nutmeg
6 tablespoons flour
1/2 cup mashed potatoes
3 tablespoons melted butter

Combine all ingredients except butter in a blender and blend well; scrape sides and blend again for 10 seconds. Add butter and blend until mixed. You may also combine all ingredients in a mixing bowl with a whisk or mixer. Pour enough batter to thinly cover bottom of hot, oiled skillet. Cook about 1 minute or until light brown on one side; flip and cook other side until brown.

Whole-Wheat Crêpes

1-1/4 cups milk
3 eggs
1/8 teaspoon salt

1 cup whole-wheat flour
Vegetable oil for frying

Combine all ingredients, except oil. Pour about 2 or 3 tablespoonfuls of batter into a hot, oiled skillet, tilting until batter covers the bottom of the pan. Cook about 1 minute or until brown; flip crêpe and cook the other side for about 30 seconds.

Crêpe Fillings

Crêpes can be served for breakfast, lunch, dinner, or dessert depending on the filling. The combinations are endless, so experiment and enjoy!

For simple fillings try: butter and jam; butter, sugar, and lemon juice; mashed berries and sugar; sour cream and brown sugar; or preserves mixed with rum or brandy.

For a heartier meal try: meats, vegetables, or seafood in a basic cream sauce. Leftover bits of meat and vegetables taste great wrapped in a crêpe.

Apple Filling

1/4 cup orange juice
1 teaspoon cornstarch
1/8 teaspoon nutmeg

2 cups peeled, chopped apples
2 tablespoons vanilla yogurt
1/8 teaspoon orange extract

Combine all ingredients except yogurt and orange extract in a saucepan. Cook, stirring occasionally, until apples are soft and sauce is thick. Place 3 tablespoonfuls of filling on each crêpe and roll up. Combine yogurt and orange extract and top each crêpe with the mixture. Makes enough to fill 8 crêpes.

Apricot Brandy Crêpes

12 crêpes
1/2 cup apricot jam
2 tablespoons melted butter
2 tablespoons sugar
1/4 cup apricot brandy

Spread crêpes with the jam; roll up and place in a buttered baking dish. Brush with melted butter and sprinkle with sugar. Broil until light brown. Heat brandy and pour over crêpes. Ignite brandy carefully. Serve immediately.

Italian Crêpes

Filling

1 cup ricotta cheese
2 tablespoons grated Parmesan cheese
1/8 teaspoon salt
1/8 teaspoon pepper
3/4 teaspoon crushed oregano

Sauce

2 tablespoons butter
2 teaspoons flour
1 cup tomato sauce

To make filling: Combine all filling ingredients and mix well. Spoon mixture onto crêpes and fold into triangles. Place in a baking dish and top with the sauce. Fills 8 crêpes. **To make sauce:** Combine butter and flour in a small saucepan, cooking and stirring until smooth, about 30 seconds. Add the tomato sauce and cook for 5 more minutes. Spoon over crêpes, then broil until brown.

Potato Filling with Parmesan Cheese

3 tablespoons vegetable oil for frying
1/2 pound potatoes, cooked and diced
Dash of salt and pepper

1/4 cup melted butter
1-1/2 tablespoons chopped parsley
1 cup grated Parmesan cheese

Heat oil in a skillet and fry potatoes until crispy brown. Remove to paper towels and season with salt and pepper. Spoon potatoes into center of each crêpe; roll up and place in a baking dish. Combine remaining ingredients and sprinkle over the crêpes. Broil until golden.

Raspberry Filling

1 (10-ounce) package frozen
   raspberries, thawed
2/3 cup water

1-1/2 tablespoons sugar
1 tablespoon cornstarch
2 tablespoons water

Drain the raspberries and put the liquid in a saucepan with 2/3 cup of water and the sugar. Bring to a boil. Dissolve cornstarch in 2 tablespoons of water and add to the boiling mixture, cooking and stirring until mixture thickens. Carefully add the raspberries. Makes about 1-1/2 cups of filling. Also great as a pancake topping.

Scallop Mushroom Crêpes

1 cup white wine	4 tablespoons butter
2 cups chicken broth	5 tablespoons flour
2 celery stalks, cut into chunks	3/4 cup milk
3 green onions, sliced	2 egg yolks, slightly beaten
2 bay leaves	1/2 cup cream
10 peppercorns	1 teaspoon lemon juice
1/2 pound mushrooms, sliced	Dash of salt
2 pounds scallops, cut in half	1-1/2 cups grated Swiss cheese

Combine wine, broth, celery chunks, green onions, bay leaves, and peppercorns. Bring to a boil and simmer for 15 minutes, then pour through a strainer into a 12-inch skillet. Discard vegetables. Return broth to a simmer and add mushrooms and scallops; simmer for about 7 minutes. Remove mushrooms and

continued

Scallop Mushroom Crêpes *continued*

scallops and boil broth until only 1 cup remains. In a saucepan, melt the butter and stir in the flour. Cook over medium heat for a few minutes, stirring constantly. Stir in the milk and the broth; continue stirring until sauce boils and thickens. In a bowl, beat egg yolks and cream; gradually add 3 tablespoonfuls of the hot broth mixture to the egg yolks; then add the egg yolk mixture to the saucepan with the hot broth. Bring to a boil; remove from heat; stir in the lemon juice and salt. Drain the scallops and mushrooms; discard the liquid. Add about half of the sauce and 3/4 cup of the cheese to the mushrooms and scallops to make the filling. Fill 12 crêpes with the filling; fold into desired shape and place seam side down in a large, greased baking dish. Pour remaining sauce over the crêpes and sprinkle with remaining cheese. Bake at 400° for about 10 minutes.

White Wine Chicken Crêpes

2 tablespoons butter
1 tablespoon minced garlic
3 pounds chicken breasts
1/8 teaspoon salt
Dash of pepper
1/2 cup chicken broth

1/2 cup white wine
1/2 tablespoon minced parsley
3/4 tablespoon crushed tarragon
1 cup cream
3 egg yolks

In a large saucepan, melt the butter; add the garlic. Add remaining ingredients except the cream and egg yolks. Cover and simmer until chicken is done. Remove the chicken; cool. Remove meat from bones and cut into bite-sized pieces. Set aside. Slowly stir the cream and egg yolks into the hot broth and cook, stirring constantly until broth is thickened. Fill about 15 crêpes with the chicken and a tablespoonful of sauce. Fold into desired shape. Arrange in a baking pan and cover crêpes with the hot broth. Bake at 350° for 15 minutes.

Zucchini Crêpes

3 tablespoons chopped onion
4 tablespoons butter, divided
1-1/2 pounds zucchini, sliced
1/2 cup chicken broth or water

1 egg
1 cup grated Cheddar cheese
12 crêpes
1/2 cup fresh bread crumbs

Sauté onion in 2 tablespoons melted butter. Add zucchini and broth. Cover and cook for about 10 minutes or until zucchini is done. Remove zucchini and onions to a mixing bowl and mix until the zucchini is broken up. Drain any liquid from the bowl. Add the egg and cheese; mix well. Spoon the zucchini filling onto crêpes; fold into desired shape. Mix remaining 2 tablespoons of butter and the bread crumbs and sprinkle over the crêpes. Bake at 350° for about 15 minutes.

Toppings and Syrups

Fruit Syrup

1/2 cup lemon juice
3-1/2 cups berries or other chopped
    fresh fruit
1 package pectin

1 cup water
1 cup light corn syrup
1-1/2 cups sugar

Put lemon juice and fruit in a blender and mix until smooth. Transfer the mixture to a saucepan and sprinkle the pectin over the fruit; stir. Let stand for half an hour. Add the water, corn syrup, and sugar. Cook until all of the sugar is dissolved. Cool. Store in jars in the refrigerator.

Blueberry Cinnamon Syrup

4 cups blueberries
3/4 cup corn syrup
1/2 teaspoon cinnamon

2 tablespoons cornstarch
1 cup water

Combine all ingredients and cook over medium heat until thickened.

Blueberry Sauce

4 tablespoons flour
1/4 cup water
2 cups fresh blueberries
1 cup sugar

Dash of salt
1-1/4 cups water
1 tablespoon lemon juice

Combine flour and water, then add all ingredients, except lemon juice; let stand about 5 minutes. Cook over medium heat until sauce boils. Stir in lemon juice. Remove from heat and cool 20 minutes. Serve warm. —*Oregon Blueberry Association*

Lemon Applesauce

2 cups applesauce
1 lemon, sliced thin, with peel
Juice of 1 lemon

3 tablespoons raisins
1/8 teaspoon nutmeg
1/2 teaspoon cinnamon

Combine all ingredients in a saucepan. Cook over medium heat until lemons are tender. Chill and serve.

Apple Cinnamon Sauce

6-1/2 cups peeled, cored, sliced apples
1 teaspoon cooking oil

1/2 cup apple cider
3/4 teaspoon cinnamon

In a skillet, cook the apple slices in the oil until tender. Add the cider and cinnamon and cook until sauce thickens slightly. Serve warm.

Brandy Maple Syrup

2 cups maple syrup   3 tablespoons melted butter
4 tablespoons brandy

Combine all ingredients. Heat and serve.

Orange Maple Syrup

3 cups maple syrup   2 tablespoons grated orange zest

Combine ingredients in a saucepan and bring to a boil. Reduce heat and simmer about 5 minutes. Serve warm.

Brown Sugar Syrup

1 pound brown sugar   1/2 cup butter
1-3/4 cups water

Combine sugar and water and boil for 3 or 4 minutes. Add butter. Serve warm.

Orange Honey Syrup

1 cup orange juice   1/3 cup butter
1-1/3 cups honey   1/2 tablespoon lemon juice

Combine all ingredients and heat to the desired temperature; serve warm.

Belgian Cream

1 cup whipping cream
1/4 cup brown sugar

1/4 teaspoon cardamom
1/3 cup sour cream

Beat cream, sugar, and cardamom until soft peaks form. Fold in the sour cream. Serve. Great on a Belgian waffle.

Cinnamon Sour Cream Sauce

1 cup sour cream
1 teaspoon cinnamon
2 tablespoons sugar (white or brown)

1/2 teaspoon vanilla
1 tablespoon grated orange or lemon
  zest (optional)

Combine all ingredients and serve.

Honey Butter

1 cup butter   1/2 cup honey

Combine and beat until light and fluffy.

Banana Honey Butter

3 mashed bananas   2-1/2 tablespoons butter, softened
4 tablespoons honey   1/2 teaspoon cinnamon (optional)

Combine all ingredients and mix until smooth.

Honey Spread

1 cup honey   1 cup sour cream

Combine and beat until light and fluffy. Store in the refrigerator.

Butterscotch Sauce

1/2 cup evaporated milk   Dash of salt
1/4 cup butter   3/4 teaspoon vanilla
2 cups dark brown sugar

Combine and cook all ingredients, except vanilla, in a double boiler for about 15 minutes. Stir in vanilla; serve warm.

Chocolate Sauce

3/4 cup sugar   3/4 cup cocoa
1 cup water or brewed coffee   1/2 teaspoon vanilla

Combine sugar and water or coffee in a small saucepan. Cook and stir until sugar dissolves; boil for 2 minutes. Add the cocoa; return to a boil, stirring constantly until smooth. Remove from heat; stir in vanilla. Serve warm.

Ham and Corn Topping

1 large can cream-style corn   3/4 cup diced ham

Combine ingredients and heat thoroughly. Great on pancakes and waffles for a brunch, lunch, or dinner.

Meat Topping

1-1/2 cups ground beef   1/4 teaspoon salt
1 small onion, chopped   1/4 teaspoon pepper
2 tablespoons tomato purée   1/4 teaspoon thyme
1-1/2 tablespoons apple cider

Brown the beef; add the chopped onions and sauté until tender. Add the remaining ingredients and mix well. Spoon the filling onto the pancakes and roll up, or serve on waffles for a delicious dinner.

Notes

Notes

Notes

Notes

BOOKS BY MAIL Penfield Stocking Stuffers: You may mix titles. Retail for $6.95 each or postpaid: One book for $10.95; 2 for $18; 3 for $25; 4 for $30; 6 for $45; 12 for $80. Complete catalog of all titles $2.50. *(Prices and availability subject to change.)* Please call 1-800-728-9998.

Æbleskiver and More (Danish)
Dandy Dutch Recipes
Dutch Style Recipes
Dear Danish Recipes
Fine Finnish Foods
German Style Recipes
Great German Recipes
Norwegian Recipes
Scandinavian Holiday Recipes
Scandinavian Smorgasbord Recipes
Scandinavian Style Fish and Seafood Recipes
Scandinavian Sweet Treats
Splendid Swedish Recipes
Time-Honored Norwegian Recipes
Waffles, Flapjacks, Pancakes
Slavic Specialties
Pleasing Polish Recipes
Cherished Czech Recipes

Czech & Slovak Kolaches & Sweet Treats
Quality Czech Mushroom Recipes
Quality Dumpling Recipes
Amish Mennonite Recipes & Traditions
American Gothic Cookbook
Recipes from Ireland
Recipes from Old Mexico
Savory Scottish Recipes
Ukrainian Recipes
Tales from Texas Tables
Texas Cookoff

License to Cook Series:
Italian Style; Texas Style;
Alaska Style; Arizona Style;
Iowa Style; Minnesota Style;
New Mexico Style; Oregon Style;
Wisconsin Style

PENFIELD BOOKS • 215 BROWN STREET • IOWA CITY, IA 52245-5801 • WWW.PENFIELDBOOKS.COM